BURNING AT STAKE

IN THE

UNITED STATES

A record of the public burning by mobs
of five men, during the first five
months of 1919, in the states
of Arkansas, Florida,
Georgia, Missis-
sippi, and
Texas

First published by the
NATIONAL ASSOCIATION FOR THE ADVANCEMENT
OF COLORED PEOPLE
June. 1919

LYNCHING PAMPHLETS

President Wilson's Lynching and Mob Violence Pronouncement (of July 26, 1918).

Lynchings of May, 1918, in Brooks and Lowndes Counties, Georgia; an investigation by the N. A. A. C. P.; 8 pages.

The Massacre of East St. Louis; an account of an Investigation by **W. E. Burghardt Du Bois** and **Martha Gruening**, for the N. A. A. C. P., illustrated, 20 pages, reprinted from *The Crisis*, for September, 1917.

The Burning of Ell Person at Memphis, Tenn.; an account taken from the Memphis daily papers of May 22, 23, 24 and June 3, 1917; 4 pages.

The Burning of Ell Person at Memphis, Tenn.; an investigation by James Weldon Johnson for the N. A. A. C. P.; reprinted from *The Crisis*, for July, 1917; 8 pages.

The Lynching of Anthony Crawford (at Abbeville, S. C., October 21, 1916). Article by **Roy Nash** (then) Secretary, N. A. A. C. P.; reprinted from the *Independent* for December, 1916; 4 pages, large size.

Thirty Years of Lynching in the United States, 1889-1918, April, 1919; 105 pages, fifty cents.

FOREWORD

In the first five months of 1919, five men were publicly burned by mobs in the United States, before crowds of from 150 to 1,500 people. Women and children watched two of the burnings and witnessed the torture meted out to the victims. It is generally conceded that one, at least, of the five men was innocent of the crime with which he was charged.

The states in which the burnings occurred are:

> **Arkansas**
> **Florida**
> **Georgia**
> **Mississippi**
> **Texas**

In none of these states has any participant in the public burning of a United States citizen been punished. Only in Texas were proceedings begun by the attorney general after a grand jury had declined to indict the murderers.

Believing that torture of human beings in public, invasion of courts and contempt for law, the release of primitive bestiality in the rule of mob passion, constitute a grave danger to civilization in the United States, the National Association for the Advancement of Colored People presents the record which follows of the five public murders by burning and of certain published comments upon those murders.

I

THE BURNING OF LLOYD CLAY

Vicksburg, Mississippi, May 14

(Headlines and news excerpts reprinted from the Vicksburg (Miss.), Evening Post, May 14, 1919.)

DOGS GET WRONG MAN!
WILL MAKE NEW START.

Lloyd Clay, young negro, about 22 years old, was arrested at the A. and V. Station as the result of a second hunt with the bloodhounds.

Brought before Miss Hudson, she declared he was not the man who attacked her last night.

Clay will be held pending further investigation. Sheriff Scott will likely have the bloodhounds put on the trail again this afternoon.

MOB SURROUNDS JAIL!
ARMED, MAKE THREATS.

When it was known that a negro had been arrested in the attempted rape of Miss Mattie Hudson, a mob surrounded the Warren jail.

Many were armed and threats were made as to the fate of the prisoner, should he prove to be guilty. Cherry and Grove Streets were lined with automobiles and men crowded the sidewalks. Chief R. G. Groome thinks the wrong man has been caught.

(*Headlines and excerpts reprinted from the Vicksburg Weekly Herald, Friday, May 16, 1919.*)

NEGRO LYNCHED AND BURNED BY MOB
Mob Overpowers Sheriff Scott and Lynches Negro

Between 800 and 1,000 men, Enraged at Series of Intrusions in Homes During Last Three Weeks Stormed the Jail and Took the Prisoner

---

NEGRO WAS CHARGED WITH ATTEMPT TO VIOLATE YOUNG WHITE GIRL AND WAS TRAILED BY BLOODHOUNDS

Mob Worked Quickly, Breaking Steel Bars with Railroad Iron—Clay Asked for a Minute to Tell Name of Other Negro but was Rushed to Clay and Farmer Streets, Strung up and Body Roasted—Number of Women Followed the Mob

---

. . . When the body was hoisted up from the ground, coal oil was poured upon the negro's head, and a match applied. The negro's hands were loose when he was strung up, and he hegan to climb up the rope, but he was lowered and his hands tied.

As the mob moved from the jail to the scene of the lynching, a number of women joined the procession and witnessed the proceedings.

(*From the first page of the Vicksburg Evening Post, May 15, 1919.*)

NEGRO TORTURED, BUT SUFFERED SILENTLY

Tormented by the flames which lapped his legs and reached to his trunk, strangled by the noose, his limbs jerked from below, Lloyd Clay, young negro of 24 years, made no outcry.

He lifted his arms, placed his palms together in an attitude of prayer, but made no sound.

As the flames burned higher, he raised his legs doubling them up in a vain effort to escape the blaze.

The mob, taking the negro from the jail shortly before 8 o'clock last night as the man guilty of attempted criminal assault upon Miss Mattie Hudson, was placed on a truck and rushed around the corner of Clay Street turning East.

A howling mob followed. The truck was loaded with men who shrieked their delight in having the man in their possession at last.

Probably two dozen automobiles followed. Others quickly arrived.

GIRL IDENTIFIES NEGRO

In the meantime a delegation had gone for Miss Hudson, They brought her to the corner of Farmer and Clay Streets where the party met the negro and his escort of many hundreds.

In a moment the corner was blocked with cars and human beings.

Shouts, howls, and the screech of motor horns made a deafening sound.

In the midst of this confusion the men brought Clay to Miss Hudson.

"Is that the man?" they asked.

"Say the word," shouted others.

She gave her decision and a thunderous shout went up.*

NEGRO STRIPPED, BEATEN

The mob fell upon the negro, snatching away his clothes and beating him. He was dragged further toward First North.

"Shall we do it?" asked a big man of the crowd.

The answer came in one long continued cheer of approval.

Three men climbed an elm tree directly in front of Mrs. Ida M. Keefe's residence. When a stout rope came into view the mob went wild.

Men from below attempted to tie Clay to the rope but failed to make a good noose. The negro was hauled up five feet and then clipped back.

The sight of the nude body rising above the crowd increased the excitement.

Another attempt was made and soon the negro was hanging by the neck from a good strong limb of the tree.

"Shoot him," some one called.

"No, No," came the answer. "Let him die slow."

"DIE SLOW," IS CRY

The negro, with head twisted, dangled limply from the line.

Seeing that Clay was merely suffering discomfort, men below began to jerk his legs.

Others smeared kerosene upon the body while others prepared a bonfire below, saturating the material with gasoline.

When the fire was touched off a grewsome sight was revealed.

---

* Confronted with the frenzied mob Miss Hudson recanted her statement of the morning, deliberately made, that Clay was not the man who had attacked her. "She recognized his clothes, she afterwards told her relatives, and seeing Clay's side face she recognized him as the man who grappled with her in her room that morning." It was known in Vicksburg that Miss Hudson's identification had been forced from her by the mob whiich was intent on having its sport with Lloyd Clay.

The flesh on the body began to crinkle and blister. The face of the negro became horribly distorted with pain. He assumed an attitude of prayer, raising his hands' palms togehther.

Some one in the rear of the crowd fired a pistol into the air.

Three seconds later firearms were popping on all sides. Even women were seen to shoot revolvers.

* * * * *

Stray bullets struck two onlookers, Benny Stafford, who suffered a wound in the chin, and an old man, Charles Lancaster, who will likely die.

The wounding of the bystanders did not detract interest from the central figure in the ghastly episode.

The fusilade of shots kept up for several minutes, then the crowd began a hubbub of gloating over the wretched form shrivelling mummy-like on the rope.

A can of gasoline was thrown on the blaze and this burned brightly for thirty minutes. The lower part of the body was thoroughly crisped, the feet burned off and a large part of the carcass charred.

The legs of the corpse curled backward grewsomely. The flesh fell off and the knee-bones showed through.

ROPE SOUVENIRS IN DEMAND

The grizzly form was allowed to dangle for an hour and a half in the moonlight.

People came and went. Men of all classes, women and even children visited the scene. The whole affair had been witnessed by many ladies who followed the mob from the jail and others who joined the crowd on the terraces nearby.

"Have you had enough fun, boys?" a leader asked.

"Yes, cut him down," came the answering shout.

When the body fell to the gutter there was a great rush for bits of rope as souvenirs.

WANT GALLOWS TREE
CUT DOWN BY CITY

The tree on which Lloyd Clay was hanged will be cut down by the city, at the request of residents of the neighborhood of Clay and Farmer Streets.

Mrs. Ida M. Keefe, living in the house in front of which the hanging took place, is particularly desirous that this be done.

"I understand it is customary," she said, "and I am sure I don't want the tree standing there after what happened last night."

"Madam," replied a man standing near who overheard her remark, "that tree is a monument to the spirit of the manhood of this community who will not tolerate crimes against their women folks.

"What was done here last night was done for you and for every woman and girl in Warren County."

Editorial Comment

(*From the Vicksburg Herald, May 16, 1919.*)

It is well for it to be known at home and abroad that this evil condition is aggravated if not provoked by such movements as the "negro country-wide campaign for equal rights," published in the New York press dispatches yesterday. Together they make a mock of policies and declarations of a better race relationship. One more kindly and just all may strive for. But never in the way of race equality in political and civil rights as this New York race propaganda calls for. That mischievous publication has acted like oil on fire, in this instance where the crime was certain and the criminal likewise. Under the same condition and circumstances the negro would have been lynched in Lincoln, Illinois.

(*From Vardaman's Weekly, May 15, 1919.*)

. . . It is hypocritical for you to denounce it. You may regret it, but if it were your daughter who had been outraged you would lead the mob.

It is said that the young woman assaulted was not able to definitely and surely identify the man who was killed as the man who made the attempted assault upon her. But negroes have been guilty of a series of crimes of this character and the infuriated mob demanded a victim upon which to wreck their revenge.

O, it is horrible! Deplorable! Regrettable! But, as I have so often said, it is going to happen as often as rapes happen, and I do not know but that the mob is the only protection to the white man's home.

Every community in Mississippi ought to organize and the organization should be led by the bravest and best white men in the community. And they should pick out these suspicious characters—those military, French-women-ruined negro soldiers and let them understand that they are under surveillance, and that when crimes similar to this one are committed, take care of the individual who commits the crime.

There is no doubt but that hell will be to pay in this country in the near future, even more than the present—and a high sense of prudence demands that the white people be prepared and ready to take care of the situation.

(*From the Vicksburg Evening Post, May* 15, 1919.)

... The terrors of mob rule were clearly exemplified in the reign of lawlessness which followed the lynching of the negro in Clay Street last night.

In the heart of the residential district, the mob members drew their weapons and fired indiscriminately in every direction. That numerous deaths of spectators and nearby residents did not result was no fault of the recklessness of the men who had taken the law into their own hands.

A Query Unacknowledged

May 19, 1919.

Hon. Theodore G. Bilbo, Governor,
    Jackson, Miss.

As you are aware, Lloyd Clay, Negro, was burned to death in a thickly populated section of Vicksburg in the presence of approximately 1,000 people, many of whom were women who, according to press accounts, looked on in silence; further that thousands viewed the body roasting over the fire and then went home.

The National Association for the Advancement of Colored People, devoting itself to an endeavor to stamp out lynching, strongly condemns the crime with which this Negro was charged, but points out that the girl did not identify Clay as her assailant. But whether guilty or not, as President Wilson says, "No man who really cares for America's fame and honor or who is truly loyal to her institutions, can justify mob action, while the courts of justice are open and the governments of the states are ready and able to do their duty." The city of Vicksburg and the State of Mississippi are now confronted with the question are the courts of your state ready and able to do their duty. That duty, we most respectfully suggest, is clear. It is that the lynchers and burners of this Negro be brought to trial in your courts.

Recently a National Conference on Lynching in New York condemned lynching; the Southern Sociological Congress at Knoxville, Tennessee, also condemned the practice, as did the Federal Council of Churches of Christ in America, meeting in Cleveland. These three great organizations, therefore, in addition to the President of the United States, challenge the city of Vicksburg and the State of Mississippi to show to the nation that law and order reign in Mississippi. Such crimes as were charged against the victim of this lynching are the crimes of degenerates. What can be said of a thousand people who stand and watch a human being burned to death.

If there is anything you care to say for the information of our press service, we shall be pleased to convey your message to the country.

                JOHN R. SHILLADY, *Secretary,*
    NATIONAL ASSOCIATION FOR THE ADVANCEMENT
              OF COLORED PEOPLE

II

THE BURNING OF BRAGG WILLIAMS

Hillsboro, Texas, January 20, 1919

(Headlines and news matter reprinted from Austin American, January 20, 1919.)

NEGRO PAYS PENALTY OF FEARFUL CRIME ON FLAMING PYRE

Bragg Williams Meets Death by Infuriated Texans Day He was Sentenced to Hang

OFFICERS OF LAW WERE OVERPOWERED

Dozens of Women and Children Looked on as Man Burned; Hillsboro, in Turmoil

Bragg Williams, negro, under death sentence for the murder of Mrs. George Wells and her child at Itasca, was taken from the Hill County jail here at noon today by a mob and burned at the stake.

The crowd was orderly and there was little excitement.

APPEAL WAS FILED

Notice of appeal from the sentence was filed by Willaims' attorneys today, and this action is said to have led the mob to taking the case into its own hands.

Mrs. Wells and her child were found murdered in their home near Itasca on December 2, 1918.

Williams was arrested on the day of the murder and spirited away to avoid threatened violence.

CONVICTED LAST WEEK

The negro was convicted of the murders here last week and taken to Dallas for safe keeping.

Texas rangers, who guarded the court room during the trial, brought Williams back from Dallas last night and lodged him in jail, after which the rangers left Hillsboro.

TO BE HANGED TODAY

This morning Williams was taken before Judge Horton Porter and sentenced to be hanged on February 21.

Attorneys for the defendant immediately filed notice of appeal.

This is said to have enraged residents of the Itasca neighborhood present, who numbered several score.

JUDGE LYNCH THERE

A mob was organized and took the law into its own hands.

County officers attempted vainly to control the crowd but it proceeded quietly to cut down a telephone pole which was used as a battering ram with which the jail door was broken in. The guards inside the jail were then rushed, the negro seized and taken to the public square where he was tied to a post.

Boxes, barrels and other fuel matter over which oil had been scattered furnished the pyre.

WOMEN AS ONLOOKERS

Between 300 and 400 persons, including dozens of women, looked on as the negro burned.

The body was entirely consumed in about forty minutes, after which the crowd quietly dispersed.

(From the Dallas Morning News, January 21, 1919.)

... The negro was brought out and led to the public square. Williams was chained to the concrete "safety post" on the square. Hay, wood, and coal were piled about him and over the mass was poured several gallons of coal oil. Then a match was applied. Williams lived but a few minutes in the flames, probably not more than five. He is said to have made no outcry at his fate further than to say "Help me, Cap," three times. While a great many persons gathered around the burning negro, business was not suspended and there was very little excitement.

(From the Houston Post, January 21, 1919.)

SAYS RANGERS DID DUTY

... Adjutant General Harley, Tuesday disclaimed the inference in the report that Bragg Williams, the negro who was burned at the stake at Hillsboro by a mob, had been deserted by the rangers. General Harley said the rangers were sent to Hillsboro at the request of the district judge to protect the negro throughout the trial. After the trial they took the negro to Dallas and put him in jail at that place and returned to Hillsboro, where the judge thanked them for their services, General Harley stated. He did not know how the negro got back to Hillsboro.

(*From the Galveston News, February 21, 1919.*)
HILL COUNTY GRAND JURY FAILS TO RETURN "LYNCHING" BILLS.

. . . The grand jury of Hill County, which has been in session at Hillsboro, adjourned finally yesterday without returning any bills of indictments against persons who participated in the mob that burned Bragg Williams, negro, in the town of Hillsboro on January 20th, last. Information to that effect was received today by Attorney General C. M. Cureton from the county attorney of Hill County.

The court of criminal appeals has not yet issued an order in the proceedings instituted yesterday by the attorney general for having twelve persons cited to appear before that court and show cause why they should not be punished for contempt of court. Contention is made by the attorney general that the members of the mob that lynched the negro Williams were in contempt of the court of criminal appeals because Williams had appealed from the judge of the trial court, which had found him guilty of murder and assessed punishment at death, thereby placing his case within the jurisdiction of the higher court.

The penalty in cases of contempt before the court of criminal appeals is fine or jail imprisonment, or both, without limitation.

A Query Unacknowledged

January 21, 1919.

Hon. W. P. Hobby, Governor,
    Austin, Tex.

Press dispatches of January Twentieth report lynching of Bragg Williams accused of murder who was taken from jail at Hillsboro, Texas, by mob and burned to death in public square. National Association for Advancement of Colored People, speaking in name of its one hundred sixty-five branches and forty-five thousand members in thirty-eight states of the Union, respectfully requests information regarding any steps being taken or contemplated by Texas authorities to uphold her laws against members of mob who have so outrageously flouted them. Since the United States entered the war to make the world safe for democracy more than one hundred Negroes have been lynched. Since President Wilson appealed to the country against lynching on July twenty-sixth, 1918, asking the governors of the states, law officers and men and women of every community in the United States to keep America's name without stain or reproach and to make an end of this disgraceful evil, twenty-one Negroes have been lynched, four of them in Texas. We urge that you use every power at your command to see that members of mob are apprehended and punished to full extent of law.

JOHN R. SHILLADY, *Secretary*,
NATIONAL ASSOCIATION FOR ADVANCEMENT
OF COLORED PEOPLE

III

THE BURNING OF BENNY RICHARDS
Warrenton, Georgia, May 2, 1919

(From United Press Dispatch to the Baltimore Daily Herald, May 3, 1919.)

NEGRO FARMER, CHARGED WITH KILLING HIS WIFE AND SHOOTING FOUR WHITE MEN, LYNCHED AT WARRENTON, GEORGIA

... Benny Richards, Negro farmer who shot his divorced wife and wounded her sister and four white men, was captured by a posse today in a swamp near here. He was immediately hanged and his body riddled with bullets. The Negro's body was then brought here and burned in the presence of three hundred people.

The Negro was captured after he had been wounded in a gun duel with the posses.

So far as is known there were no officers of the law present when Richards was captured, when he was hanged and shot, or when he was burned.

Large quantities of gasoline was poured on the shallow waters of the swamp and set afire as one means of driving the fugitive black into the open.

(From the East Tennessee News, May 15, 1919.)

... His body was then burned before a crowd of 300 who took off a day's holiday in order to be in at the "killing,"

A Query Unacknowledged

May 3, 1919.

Hon. Hugh M. Dorsey, Governor,
    Atlanta, Georgia

    On eve of assembling of National Conference on Lynching, upon call of more than one hundred twenty citizens of all sections of country, one of them yourself, Georgia mob lynched Negro, Benny Richards, riddled his body with bullets, and then burned it in presence of three hundred people, according to press dispatches, lynched victim being accused of killing his wife and wounding her sister and four white men. National Association for Advancement of Colored People urges you to demand that legal authorities proceed energetically to ascertain identity of lynchers, indict them and bring them to trial. Mob worked in daytime. It should be possible to identify them.

JOHN R. SHILLADY, *Secretary*,
NATIONAL ASSOCIATION FOR THE ADVANCEMENT OF COLORED PEOPLE

IV

THE BURNING OF FRANK LIVINSTON
Eldorado, Arkansas, May 21, 1919

(From the New York Evening Post, May 22, 1919.)

BURNED TO DEATH BY MOB

Whites and Negroes Take Part in Arkansas Lynching

... Frank Livinston, negro, was tied to a tree and burned to death by a mob of about 150 men, both white and negroes, about eighteen miles from here, yesterday afternoon. It is said that the negro confessed that he killed his employer and latter's wife, Mr. and Mrs. Robinson Clay, Tuesday night, after he had quarrelled with Clay. Their charred bodies were found later in the ruins of their home.

A mob was immediately formed, including many negroes, which captured Livinston. Sheriff Craig and a posse, who attempted to prevent the lynching, arrived just a few minutes too late. No arrests were made. Livinston recently was discharged from the army at Camp Pike.

A Query Unacknowledged

May 23, 1919.

Hon. Charles Brough, Governor,
    Little Rock, Ark.

National Association for Advancement of Colored People, speaking in behalf of its two hundred ten branches and fifty-four thousand members of both races in thirty-nine states, respectfully requests information concerning steps being taken or proposed by Arkansas authorities to deal with lynchers of Frank Livinston, Negro, recently discharged from United States Army who, according to press dispatches, was tied to a tree and burned to death by mob near Eldorado, Arkansas, on May twenty-first, accused of murdering his employer and the latter's wife following a quarrel. Press dispatches state that Sheriff Craig of Union County arrived a few minutes too late to prevent the lynching but that no arrests were made.

This is the second lynching to occur in your state within thirty days, in both of which cases the crime charged was murder for which the laws of Arkansas provide ample punishment. May we suggest that you as a professed leader of Southern liberal opinion, as former President of the Southern Sociological Congress which ten days ago passed strong resolutions against lynching, and as former Chairman of the Southern University Race Commission which also has condemned lynching, have a special duty as a man no less than as Governor to proceed energetically in defense of the laws of your state and in condemnation of the barbarity which is increasingly disgracing America.

JOHN R. SHILLADY, *Secretary,*

NATIONAL ASSOCIATION FOR THE ADVANCEMENT
OF COLORED PEOPLE

V

THE BURNING OF JUDGE JOHNSON
Castleberry, Florida, March 4, 1919

(Headline and news item reprinted from the Chicago Plaindealer, March 22, 1919.)

MOB BURNS ONE

... A delegation of prominent citizens called on the county officers early today. They informed them that they composed a reception committee appointed to entertain Judge Johnson, a gentleman of color, in their custody. The county officers claimed that he was a prisoner charged with having attacked a white woman and had confessed. The delegation demanded that he be turned over to them. The officers refused, so the delegation proceeded to "take" Johnson away from them, which was neatly done without the loss of a single life or gunshot. It is needless to say that the delegation proceeded to "entertain" Johnson, who, without any undue ceremony, was burned to death.

Two Letters

A letter from Governor Sidney J. Catts of Florida and the Association's reply. On March 15th, the Association wired Governor Catts calling his attention to the lynching of two Negroes, Bud Johnson and Joe Walker, and asked that the lynchers be brought to justice.

March 18, 1919.

JOHN R. SHILLADY, Secretary,
  National Association for Advancement of Colored People.
Sir:
  I have your telegram, calling my attention to the lynching of two negroes in this State.
  As you doubtless know I have exerted every effort possible to keep down lynching in this State. I was not cognizant of the lynching at Madison until I saw an account of it in the papers. In regard to the one at Milton. I was called up at midnight and told about the crime committed by this man and had him carried to Pensacola and put in Jail there; next morning the Sheriff of Pensacola called me up and stated he was not safe there and I ordered him taken to

Montgomery and sent down to Jacksonville for safekeeping, but Sheriff Harvell was overtaken and the man punished by death at the hands of an infuriated mob from Santa Rosa County.

You ask me to see that these lynchers are brought to trial. This would be impossible to do as conditions are now in Florida, for when a negro brute, or a white man, ravishes a white woman in the State of Florida, there is no use having the people, who see that this man meets death, brought to trial, even if you could find who they are; the citizenship will not stand for it.

You state that the man in Madison was burned to death and that it adds to the horror of lynching and disgraces not only this State but the whole United States. Your race is always harping on the disgrace it brings to the State, by a concourse of white people taking revenge for the dishonoring of a white woman, when if you would spend one half the time that you do, in giving maudlin sympathy, to teaching your people not to kill our white officers and disgrace our white women, you would keep down a thousand times greater disgrace.

I do not like the tone of your telegram at all, because you tacitly commend the crime your people committed while you abuse our people for resenting the wrong which your race has done. I have tried to be fair to your people at all times but I do not believe in such maudlin sentiment as this. If any man, white or black, should dishonor one of my family he would meet my pistol square from the shoulder, and every white man in this South, who is a red-blooded American, feels the same as I do.

Therefore, you had best, as you say you are composed of 180 branches of 48,000 people in 38 States, spend some time in teaching the wanton, reckless negroes of your race, who wander from City to City, County to County and State to State, doing all the devilment that they can. We do not have any trouble from negroes who are settled, own their homes, have their own property, cattle and horses, but it is the roving, transient, irresponsible and unmarried element of tramp negroes who bring all this disgrace on the country.

I, as a representative of one million people, both white and black, urge you to send out your missionaries and get your race to stop this kind of wanton and disgraceful ravishing of the white people of the South, or the Governors of the South will not be able to keep the mobs down, which I have used every effort possible to do in Florida.

Yours very truly,

(Signed) SIDNEY J. CATTS,
Governor of Florida.

March 28, 1919.

HON. SIDNEY J. CATTS, Governor,
Tallahassee, Fla.
Sir:

I have yours of the 18th in acknowledgment, reply and criticism of my telegram of the 15th.

First, I wish to commend the attempts made by you to safeguard the prisoner at Milton. May I make it clear that in the telegram addressed to you we are not directing criticism against you as an individual but are speaking to you in your representative character as Governor of the State of Florida. Do you not think that when you ordered the sheriff of Pensacola to take his prisoner to Montgomery in order to have him sent down to Jacksonville for safe keeping, Sheriff Harvell should have known, as an experienced and responsible officer of the State, the mind of the citizenship of whom you speak in your letter and would have been prepared with sufficient officers to protect any prisoner at the hands of the mob, no matter how infuriated? The experience of Governor Stanley of Kentucky who himself protected a prisoner, and of the few other brave officers of the law, warrants the belief that mobs which form in violation of the law will not attempt to carry out their purpose if they are met with strong resistance on the part of officers of the law who realize the meaning of their oaths and are determined that prisoners shall be tried in the courts and not by mobs on the highways.

Your assertion that the citizenship of Florida will not stand for seeing men who ravish white women tried in the courts is a serious commentary on our laws. Burning to death is so horrible that we can hardly believe, if we did not read your own words, that you as Governor of a great state find it possible to apologize for burning at the stake. This Association does not apologize for crime or condone it any way. Your gratuitous assumption that I personally "tacitly commend the crime" committed is absolutely unwarranted. In order to protest against the burning of a human being at the stake, we did not feel that anyone would expect that we must begin such protest by disavowal of sympathy with the crime.

You speak a good deal about the horror of the crime. We think the crime is horrible, but we insist, as we believe all right-minded citizens of the United States are coming more and more to insist, that it is a greater crime for the governor of a state or the sheriff of a county to stand by and see the laws made by the people ignored and flouted. We do not believe that it is a justification for this lynching of the law to plead the wickedness of the criminal. Laws are made to deal with such and the question is whether in this crucial time of the world's history American states shall flaunt their disregard of law in the face of President Wilson at Paris while he is endeavoring to promote the peace of the world.

All the arguments you make about the horror of the one crime do not touch the other—the man was only accused of shooting a watchman, a crime which, certainly, it was easy to punish in the courts.

Speaking of educating, you suggest that our Association spend time teaching wanton, reckless Negroes. May I remark that as Governor of the State, you yourself take up the task of providing proportionate school facilities for the education of Negroes in your state. According to the report of the United States Bureau of Education on Negro Education, the relative per capita expenditures in Florida are; teaching white children, $11.50, and for the colored children, $2.64.

Incidentally, though it is not a point of importance, may I remark that I do not happen to be a Negro myself, as you seem to assume throughout your letter.

Sincerely yours,

(Signed) JOHN R. SHILLADY, Secretary.

A Note on Burning At Stake

We often view historical events in a dispassionate manner. It is therefore important that Black Classic Press has chosen to republish *Burning At Stake in the United States,* for it compels us to establish an emotional link with the past. *Burning At Stake in the United States* is a compilation of journalistic accounts of lynchings and burnings of Blacks by white mobs during the first five months of 1919, in Arkansas, Florida, Georgia, Mississippi, and Texas. The pamphlet was originally published by the National Association for the Advancement of Colored People (NAACP) in 1919. The NAACP used it to expose white racist violence against Blacks, and to seek judicial and legislative recourse for its victims.

Aggressive acts by whites against Blacks and the malicious destruction of human life were not peculiar to 1919. There are numerous recorded instances of Blacks being burned to death by white mobs as early as the Eighteenth and Nineteenth Centuries. A few examples will illustrate this point.

During the Eighteenth Century, whites, apprehensive about potential slave revolts, sought to maintain control of the slave population through coercion. In Newton, Long Island, in 1708, a slave revolt left seven whites dead. One Black woman was burned to death because of her participation in the revolt. In 1712, a group of slaves, again in New York, were executed for seeking freedom; several of them were burned to death. The sentence for one of the executed read, "Burned with a slow fire (so) that he may continue in torment for eight or ten hours...until he (is) dead and consumed to ashes."

In 1720, several South Carolina slaves were "hang'd and burnt" to death for seeking freedom and refuge among Africans and Native Americans in St. Augustine, Florida. Lynchings and burnings of this type continued into the Nineteenth Century. The New York Draft Riot in 1863 started as a protest against unfair conscription practices but ended in white racist violence against Blacks. White protesters marched through Black communities destroying lives and property. The protesters roasted the lifeless body of a Black man which was hung from a lamp post. The body of another Black man was mangled and burned.

With the close of the Nineteenth Century, burnings of Blacks continued unabated. In 1893, a white mob in Memphis, Tennessee, hung a Black man, Mr. Lee Walker. Ida B. Wells, in her book, *A Red Record* (1895), provides a vivid description of the brutality which accompanied the lynching:

Half a dozen men seized the naked body. The crowd cheered. They marched to the fire, and giving the body a swing, it landed in the middle of the fire. There was a cry for more wood, as the fire had begun to die owing to the long delay. Willing hands procured the wood, and it was piled upon the Negro, almost, for a time, obscuring him from view. The head was in plain view, as also were the limbs, and one arm which stood out high above the body, the elbow crooked, held in that position by a stick of wood. In a few moments the hands began to swell, then came great blisters over all exposed parts of the body; then in places the flesh was burned away and the bones began to show through.

Mob violence against Blacks often took on the veneer of a "Sunday outing," or a "festive" occasion, with hundreds of men, women, and children in attendance. In 1893, a crowd of some 10,000 people came to Paris, Texas on special trains to observe the burning of a mentally retarded Black man. Three years prior to the burnings outlined in *Burning At Stake*, 3,000 whites responded to an invitation by a Tennessee newspaper to witness the burning of a "live Negro."

These events often ended in a spree for momentoes: fragments of a hand; a dismembered leg; genitalia; a charred, brittle and disfigured ear; a piece of rope, etc. Occasionally, souvenir salesmen sold the mutilated and charred remains of lynch victims to the crowd. Bits of crushed bone were sold for twenty-five cents, thin slices of liver "crisply cooked" were sold for ten cents.

These atrocities were frequently carried out in the presence of civil authorities—the militia, police, etc. The civil authorities actively participated in some of these murderous sprees. In 1904, while two Black men were dragged from the courthouse in Statesboro, Georgia, the militia stood by docily. According to John Hope Franklin's *From Slavery to Freedom*, the militia refused to load their guns "in tender consideration of the mob." The two Black men were subsequently burned to death.

Armed Blacks often sought to confront white mobs with a readiness to protect their lives, families, and property. Under such circumstances, civil authorities usually arrested and jailed Blacks for defending themselves; other Blacks were arrested and jailed on trumped-up charges of inciting to riot. Still others were arrested as they sought refuge from mob attacks. The number of whites arrested, prosecuted, and convicted for participating in these acts of unrestrained lawlessness was negligible, less than one percent.

During the second decade of the Twentieth Century, some one-half million Black people migrated from the South, leaving the oppression of sharecropping, crop devastation, floods, and lynch mobs. Blacks congregated in developing urban areas such as Chicago, New York, and Detroit. A shortage of white labor caused by World War I and restrictions on European immigration, provided an opportunity for Blacks to find work in the factories which fueled the imperialist war effort.

Yet the conditions faced by Blacks in the North were little better than those previously confronted in the South. In 1911, Coatesville, Pennsylvania, a Black man was dragged from a local hospital by a cheering mob. Some 4,000 people participated in his lynching. The mob "...lynched him by three times thrusting him into, and withdrawing him from a roaring bonfire." In 1917, in East St. Louis, IL., white mobs, instigated by the media and organized labor, rampaged through the Black community savagely mauling and murdering Black men, women, and children. Houses were set aflame. Some Blacks died; others, badly beaten, were thrown into the burning debris.

A variety of reasons were given by whites to justify the lynching and burning of Blacks: a misguided glance, an allegation of murder, a refusal to move when demanded or a lackadaisical attitude in so doing. Yet the most prominent reason given was rape. Whites often hid their barbarous acts behind the myth of Black men impatiently waiting to ravage white women. Less than 25 percent of the Black men murdered (lynched) in the United States between 1882 and 1968 were accused of rape or attempted rape. An even smaller percentage of Black men lynched were ever tried, much less convicted of rape. The allegation of rape also fails to explain why several dozen Black women were lynched and or burned to death. The reasons are more objectively traced to systemic white racism and to the nature of capitalism.

Fortunately, Blacks developed an activist tradition (a survivalist tradition) that responded directly to white mob violence. Numerous men and women, known and unknown, contributed to this tradition, including those who struggled against overpowering odds during the period of chattel slavery. Men and women of the post-Reconstruction period such as T. Thomas Fortune advocated retaliatory self-defense in the face of mob attacks during the 1880s. By the last decade of the Nineteenth Century, he organized an anti-lynching campaign through the Afro-American League. In 1883, Henry McNeal Turner of the African Methodist Episcopal Church also mounted an anti-lynching campaign. Ida B. Wells used her journalistic expertise and the influence of her newspaper, *Free Speech*, to dispel the myths surrounding the causes of rape and lynching. She also advocated armed self-defense, emigration, and economic boycotts to eliminate mob violence. Other journalists and organizers such as W.E.B. DuBois, Monroe Trotter, and John E. Bruce were equally ardent in their opposition to white mob violence.

While *Burning At Stake* emphasizes events that transpired in 1919, it is important to remember that these events exist as part of the historical continuum of Black and white relations in the United States. As such, an awareness of this historical continuum helps to reduce one's distance from the past, a past from which we must learn. It is a past which must be remembered and never allowed to reoccur.

Kinya Kiongozi

June 1986

The KKK Meeting That Never Was
CIA Classifies Report on What Is Now Called a 'Tasteless Joke'

By George Lardner Jr.
Washington Post Staff Writer

The Central Intelligence Agency, which has recently thrust into the limelight its efforts to prevent leaks of national security information, has classified as "confidential" the details of a mock Ku Klux Klan meeting at the agency that is now being dismissed as "a tasteless joke."

The incident occurred around Christmas last year when a CIA officer and an outside consultant walked into a room called the "Ruffing Center" in the headquarters' computer services area, sources said.

According to the sources, the two were astonished at what they saw: There were perhaps 15 to 20 people in the room. Some wore cone-shaped hats made out of computer paper and they had a black man up against a wall. They appeared to be intimidating him.

After a few moments, the sources said, they let the black man go. The two interlopers asked what was going on. According to the sources, the two were told, " 'This is a Klan meeting. We're connected with the Baltimore Klavern,' or something to that effect."

Thus began what one intelligence official has described as "a tasteless joke" that got out of control. But the incident and subsequent remarks were taken seriously enough at the time that they led to complaints to the CIA inspector general and an internal investigation, and finally to inquiries from the Senate Select Committee on Intelligence.

Several weeks ago, the CIA submitted a report to intelligence committee Chairman David F. Durenberger (R-Minn.) and Vice Chairman Patrick J. Leahy (D-Vt.) but classified it as "confidential."

"I can't talk about it," Leahy said when asked about the report. "It's classified."

Durenberger said he was not familiar with the details. He said as he understood it, "There was something there, but it wasn't what it was cracked up to be."

According to the sources, the "joke" became an extended one. They said the outside consultant was asked, possibly in a subsequent discussion, whether she wanted to participate in KKK activities. She had put a note on a CIA bulletin board earlier saying she was a seamstress willing to take on some work, the sources said, and one of the putative Klansmen told her they needed robes or costumes.

The consultant, the sources continued, was also told that the purpose of the group was "to keep blacks and ethnics"—which she took to be a reference to Hispanics and Asians—"in their place."

The CIA officer with her also took the matter seriously, the sources said, and lodged a complaint. Later, when the officer asked about the status of his inquiry, he was reportedly told not to worry, that the targets of his complaint were no longer "doing anything that's dumb."

That was interpreted by some to mean that the supposed KKK unit was no longer holding meetings at agency headquarters, but CIA and Senate officials are emphatic in saying there never was a real Klan "meeting" to begin with.

"We are completely satisfied that there is not any KKK klavern or unit out there," intelligence committee aide David Holliday said for Leahy.

Under a 1982 executive order issued by President Reagan, "Information may not be classified . . . unless its disclosure reasonably could be expected to cause damage to the national security." The con-

There were 15 to 20 people in the room. Some wore cone-shaped hats made out of computer paper and they had a black man up against the wall.

fidential stamp "shall be applied to information, the unauthorized disclosure of which reasonably could be expected to cause damage to the national security."

CIA spokeswoman Kathy Pherson said, "About all I can do for you is tell you the allegations about KKK activity were made in a Vienna [Va.] newspaper . . . . I think it was sometime last month. The allegations are completely false. They were investigated by the [CIA's] inspector general and shown to be without foundation."

The allegations, however, were not aired first in a Vienna newspaper. They first appeared in an article by former CIA official Victor Marchetti in the May 12 edition of Spotlight, a right-wing weekly tabloid published in Washington. Marchetti maintained that the Klan "meeting" was real and that the CIA was apparently "attempting to stonewall the story" until it could "come up with a plausible and hopefully acceptable explanation."

Bernard F. McMahon, staff director for the intelligence committee, said he understood that the incident took place "in a small office where everybody is friendly with everybody else. I don't remember what triggered the activity, but it was something innocuous. It was not a slur or a fight or anything."

010621-400-4-60W